Soft Touch
Louise G Cole

smith|doorstop

Published 2019 by
Smith|Doorstop Books
The Poetry Business
Campo House
54 Campo Lane
Sheffield S1 2EG

Copyright © Louise G Cole 2019
All Rights Reserved

ISBN 978-1-912196-25-8

Designed and Typeset by Utter
Printed by Biddles Books

Smith|Doorstop Books are a member of Inpress: www.inpressbooks.co.uk. Distributed by NBN International, Airport Business Centre, 10 Thornbury Road Plymouth PL6 7PP

The Poetry Business gratefully acknowledges the support of Arts Council England.

Contents

5	Fur Coat and No Knickers
6	Soft Touch
8	My Sister Bakes Artisan Bread
9	The World Wide Web as a Metaphor for Love
10	Dirty Little Dresses
12	Made Up
13	Worcester, as in Source
14	Michelangelo's Nose Hair
15	Understanding Possession
16	Watermarked
17	Growing Boobs
18	Rooted
19	Strung Out
20	The Wee Girls Do Easter
21	Daze
22	Naming Petrichor
23	Instinctive Genuflection
24	Plucked
25	Beacon
26	Ways with Rotten Cabbage
28	Acknowledgements

As always, for my family, in the sense of nuclear:
David, Laurence and Rhiannon

Fur Coat and No Knickers

Drawing breath between tales of dead
        little brothers and elderly neighbours
moved away, my mother looks inside
        a lifetime that's 92 and counting,
claims no-one's visited for months,
        thinks I'm her cousin Betty
with designs on her fur coat and hopes
        of borrowing a fiver.
I try not to mind the care home smell
        and wonder what else to talk about when
the devil himself taps my shoulder
        suggests I unburden, reveal secrets
never before shared, so I offer a revelation:
        I lost my virginity four times
before I was married. She's never yet listened to me
        so it's no surprise she doesn't hear,
continues with a rattle about imagined walks
        in the park yesterday, shopping
trips she'll make next week.
        A carer comes to tuck her in,
brings weak tea and egg sandwiches,
        asks if I'd like some,
is relieved when I decline.
        I get up to leave and the frail old cripple
who used to be my mother
        spills her tea and demands
to know when cousin Betty intends returning
        the fur coat, says quietly: "I always knew
what a little whore you were."

Soft Touch

Stroking the navy-legginged thighs
of a woman who used to be me,
daydreaming at the traffic lights,
lost in the fabric feel of fantasy,

holding a freshly-minted
babe-in-arms, sleepy-wrapped
in a bunny print baby grow,
poppers snapped against wriggle;

leaning against the still-taut
muscles of a former six-pack
strained against stained singlet,
curled silver chest hair peeking;

embarrassed by smooth gussets,
newly-washed panties immodestly
teetering atop Monday's laundry
should-have-put-away-sooner pile;

hiding in a rock-chick t-shirt
faded into over-worn nightwear,
colourless soft cotton comforter
at bedtime's long, lonely stretch;

distracted by indecently tight
white boxers, clinging, I'm hot
blushing, not knowing where to
look, but I'm looking anyway;

or here's me, grey polishing cloths
formerly known as clothing, now
dusting shelves, mopping spills,
rubbing a shine onto mirrors

reflecting my life almost done.

My Sister Bakes Artisan Bread

reaching over my head for prime organic,
flours the worktop and I resist
the urge to write French curses in the dust,

stand aside as she clouts heavy, fat-lumped
dough, tries to knock it into shape with a slap,
a pinch here, a punch there.

I watch her fashionably thin shoulders shrug off
filial cares, talk to her back as she works,
try not to wince at each thump.

And all the while, sounds drift in from the road,
laden lorries heading for Tescos
with their cargo of master-baked bread.

The World Wide Web as a Metaphor for Love

Not as fake news or tweeted half-truths BTW,
but the newsfeed certainty, you have half
a zillion hits, and all your friends on Facebook
they like you, they like and like, they like you
don't they? And when there's a love interest,
pose for soft focus selfies, best angle shots,
Plenty of Fish for him, her, them, Snapchat,
Instagram, go viral with a hashtag, swell with
pride, swipe a right to light up Tinder, Google
the hot response, no real people are ever hurt
in the exchange, it's the internet, YouTube can
show you which way; email screenshots, flood
your blog with data, suggest Spotify playlists
for a broken heart when you WhatsApp, see
who is online, discover you're being ghosted,
simmered, iced, it's all good, LOL, because even
if he blocks you, TBH you're liked, you're liked,
you're liked, everyone knows, yes, you're liked.

Dirty Little Dresses

Back when you were still mine
– before school but after cradle –
we'd Wednesday walk to the village hall
puffing dragons' breath
across dim-lit benches and trestle tables,
our voices echoing bathroom-style.

At my feet, you spilled Dayglo orange squash
– the kind I wouldn't have in the house –
while I sipped something tepid and
vaguely coffee-flavoured from a plastic mug, tried
making big the small talk with other mothers.

All these years later I am surprised
at your recall of the precious poppet
pushed through the door, always dressed
in impossibly white cotton frocks, pretty, pristine
seldom up for finger painting and sandpitting.

She played quiet, solo games
emerging clean and unruffled,
remarked by a loud, proud parent
while you came back to me messy and wild,
hand painted, squashed and sandpapered.

You said you always had a thing
for her Snow Whiteness until secondary school
when she went Goth
and the dresses darkened to black,
full of salacious slashes revealing flashes
of snail-trail scars on pale flesh.

Neither of us heard what became
of the pushy mother.

Made Up

This morning's vanilla and rosemary ritual is unhurried;
today, she's tethered by the ears to a slim silver screen,
squinting into a dazzled version of herself balanced
on the denim, tight-crossed legs of youth, painting on
a face for the world to see, dabbing with plump pink
sponges, smoothing, shaping, with an artist's palette
of mascara, shadow, liner in a sparkled fabric pouch
which once held schoolgirl pens and coloured pencils.
She brushes lashes, brows, then hair, flicking, twisting,
pulling, creates a just-left-bed look that's all the rage.
Done, she gurns at her reflection, turns to see me
standing, watching in the doorway, grins: "Will I do?"

Worcester, as in Source

My sense of place still smells of Lea and Perrins
where I bore my children, two dead, two alive,
in the faithful city as tea time swans gathered
for bread shop buns, stale cakes, in the shadow
of the Cathedral, King John's thumb bone still
there in a much-fingered casket, bells loud
above willow-whack-leather of the cricket pitch.

Further along the Severn, Pitchcroft Racecourse,
when not under winter water, good for walks
or picnics, regattas or hot air balloons sailing
into a future where down and outs in shop
doorways watch fragrant ladies who lunch
order artisan-baked petit fours and canapés
for exclusive, after race, off-your-face parties.

Michelangelo's Nose Hair

During home truths and post-coital naval-gazing you say
I should understand that all there has ever been, is now,
will be forever, meaning we've already lived, will live again,
but not that we can remember or predict. It blows my mind
to think of what I am now, what I could eventually become,
or might have been: Michelangelo's nose hair, Hitler's first
moustache, fingers pressing the final apocalyptic button,
Marilyn Monroe's moist lips, my grandchildren's liver spots,
pus in a trench poet's gangrene leg, scabs on a plague rat,
entrails on a medieval butcher's block, Queen Vic's vomit –
Horse shit, you interrupt loudly, *you'll always, always be
a steaming pile of horse shit*. But you smile as you say it.

Understanding Possession

Whenever I see red, you are across the room
back turned to me, sycophantic wannabes
hanging on your every word, siren sisters
flirting, offering such wit, charm, good looks,
expensive gifts, as if any of that matters to you.

I know it shouldn't, it shouldn't, it shouldn't turn
your head, but I long for it to be me alone to hold
your gaze, keep private those secret things said
and done, deep places explored in the soft,
sticky hours before dawn, colour-drenched kicks
they'll never know of, only speculating when hints
of me float from your paintings, serenades, poems.

They might wonder at the muse who conjures
stripes of turquoise, crushed ochre, taupe,
flings them sky high, a flock of little birds to mark
a shocking summer outburst when red poppies
snagged my vision, and I raged against sharing you,
shook out my hurt, broadcast it from high places.

Watermarked

The teeming river's upright heron casts
my father: alert, slim and spike-beaked
beady-eyed in two-tone grey, topped
with a slick, black-backed comb over
feathers presented neat, formal, unruffled

observing life and love, respecting fast water
watching calmly without comment.
Unspoken childhood hardships shaped
a quiet man, stoic, strengths hidden
in patience, reserve, attention to detail

small pleasures in unusual pastimes
ships in bottles, keeping bees, Austin Sevens,
high flying kites of his own making.
Like the heron, solemn, straight and steady
taking flight only when required, just for me

on days when needy, rattled, hopeless
I catch his unexpected shape overhead,
majestic wing-beat recalling that special day
when through a single thought, so intense
with longing, need manifested a grey heron

waiting on the gatepost, regarding my arrival
with a stern look, inscrutable, but so familiar
composed, sombre, self-contained, concerned
watching calmly without comment,
I saluted, was sure I saw him almost smile.

Growing Boobs

At the deli counter in Woolworths
I dreaded the little grey pervy bloke
who came every Saturday morning

to hold my gaze with a leer, ask for
exactly seven and a half ounces
of mature farmhouse cheddar

that's what they weigh, he'd say
staring at my teenage chest as I
positioned the cheese-wire, *each*,

and I'd hurry to greaseproof wrap,
take the money without touching.
He was ahead of his time, balls of

buffalo mozzarella more suggestive,
but they hadn't yet landed in rural
Worcestershire, this was the 1970s

where we also went without broccoli,
seedless satsumas, bottled water,
duvets, skimmed milk in cartons.

I was told not to mind, take no notice,
be respectful, poor man was probably
a war hero.

Rooted

Know ten things about me,
nine of them concern the trees
the Oak, Willow, Ash, Beech,
Douglas Fir, Silver Birch, Elm,
the Twisted Hazel, Sycamore.

I hear them roar, name-calling
as they bend in the wind, angry
to be anchored to the spot
I can leave at any time, and I will
I will,
I will.

Strung Out

How long, long, long is the piece
of string tying me to your memory?
Brown paper parcels at Christmas,
birthdays, no return for the cousins'
hand-me-downs, their nearly-news;
Blue Peter Christmas glitter, cheery
tinsel-wrapped coat hangers; straight
lines plumbed for striped wallpaper;
high-flying kites of your own making,
all the beach to launch; happy, hippy
macramé plant pots in knots; tie-dyed
shirts in shades of lilac, burnt orange;
chair-back feather bundles dangled for
kitten-caper playtimes; runner-bean
wigwams, pea-sticks in a long summer,
so hot it has scratched a memory, end
of sick-bed cat's cradle games to pass
the time: was it measles, chickenpox?
All this from a ball of twisted twine
rolled from a dusty, half-forgotten drawer.

The Wee Girls Do Easter

The grannies tut disapproval of dainty girls
in dresses short enough to cause blushes
at Sunday Mass, *look now, aren't the Easter
flowers lovely, fluffy yellow chicks and ribbons?
And what chocolate we ate for breakfast!*

But there's always one – *not ours, thank God* –
bloodthirsty, curious, claims a front row seat,
clear view of the re-enactment, a stand-in only tied
to the rough-hewn wooden cross, pretending agony,
though he's caught her eye in sheepish grin.

The original drove iron nails, real gore, thunderclaps
and lightning. Now the grannies fear nightmares,
crucifixion being such an act of violence for girleens
before the Easter Bunny soothes with candy eggs,
a sugar rush beyond the churchyard gates.

But the inquisitive one holds back, stares hard,
she's taken by the tableau at the altar, lingers,
not tempted by sweet-treat promises, instead
demands to see blood, asks loud above the clatter,
Why is the half-dead man not screaming?

Daze

In a dream, my muse leans in
to kiss my open mouth, breathes

fire into my bones until I wake
hot, confused, not knowing

if he was really she, and if so,
oh, what does that make me?

No matter, it was a lovely kiss
and later I will taste a poem in it.

Naming Petrichor

Not only scent, it has colour too, slate grey
like the rain it follows, shaded vague, pastel,
puddled, brighter in moonshine, transparent
in sun, more intense than yellow-green grass
or crimson crimped flowers – and a taste,
flavoursome, pungent, at once sweet and sharp.
Sound as well, steady, ready drips dropped
deliberately, soaked earth channelling watery
overflows into streams, rivers, lakes and an
ocean separated by boasts of its own salty
lexicon, while inland, we taste that air after rain,
see it, feel it, hear it, know the special smell
is different in one place to another, yet same,
name brought from a need to label life, love,
hope in the '60s, when anything was possible
but fifty years on, I fret over what we called it
before then? We knew it, loved it, dedicated
poems to its form before ever it was titled.
Until I can award a new name in recognition
of majesty, the tingle it elicits, senses slewed
sideways by its fleeting perfumed promise,
until then, it is petrichor. Petrichor, petrichor.

Instinctive Genuflection

I tried reimagining religion but couldn't
get past flowing robes, coughs of incense,
Gregorian chants and fine silver goblets,
gold crusted altars built by broken-backed
serfs, families starved in the Big Hunger,
down-trodden women mopping the floors
of misogyny, twisting prayers into hope,
embroidered offerings for priests, spirits,
fairies, imagining the greatness of giants,
myths and legends, flame-haired witches,
bearded wizards breathing fire, brimstone,
heaven and hell manifested as suffering,
crucifixion the only approved redemption
from sin, whether original, mortal, venal,
annunciation from the Holy See hinting
at riches beyond belief to assuage the guilt
of Marian laundry girls, their immaculate
conceptions from seed spilled by blameless
boys, careless and carefree, brought up by
martyred women to venerate holy virgins,
to worship stable nativity scenes, a dying
figure nailed to a wooden cross, Christmas
angels, wings wide-spread, rosy cheeked
cherubs staring at a sacred space between
now and then; I tried reimagining religion,
couldn't get past heartbreak, lies, despair,
misunderstandings, puerile acts, blind faith.

Plucked

She knows the place where hope goes
bereft of all its feathers, stretched prostrate
on stones worn smooth from petitions
to the gods, to Allah, Jehovah, God, Oh Lord
he knows his name, she knows it too

knows she trussed the thing with string
to hold its shape, sloughed off the skin
long done with hanging, drawing, dropped
entrails to the gutter, gagged at pinkness
naked, plucked, ready to be jointed, boned

knows she's lost her grip on reason,
normality slipping away in increments
of longing and regret, imagines gristle,
sinews snapped, quivering in the half
light, half night, braced to take its weight

knows the moment when she'll belly-flop
into oblivion, teased, quills tweezed, carcass
pinioned, to lodge deep within the space
between here and there, blood red and tender,
the raw hole where once her heart beat.

Beacon

Where now is that palm-fit sea stone
we agreed was shaped as a lighthouse,
claimed from a wet Welsh holiday beach?
I ran child's fingers along its white helix,
stairs to the flashing beacon, while you

explained the principle of harbour lights
and I wondered if the keeper was lonely
alone on top of cliffs or far out at sea,
didn't know then, until it didn't matter,
white lines in grey were glinting calcite

strata in a bed of limestone exposed
by the ocean's salt water pounding,
time's rough edges all sanded smooth.
Now, another sea pebble on my desk
weighs down a tower of poems

lamenting your loss, stops the sighs
of a broken heart from blowing them
not seawards, perhaps, but elsewhere.
It's a piece of rock, but not the same
now you're gone, it's just not the same.

Ways with Rotten Cabbage

The well-dressed woman in the Costa queue
hears a culchie up to the Big Smoke for the day,
shudders in recognition of the home-place lilt,
almost hawks and spits, eyes narrow, chin lifts,
she still has poison to suck from the wounds
of a childhood there forty years ago.

In the time it takes to brew a latte she unburdens:
second of nine, ever hungry, cold and tired,
chores before school and after,
often instead of, but who cared anyway?
Idleness, TB and priests the demons to fear,
no possessions everything shared, even underwear,
shoes, skin, soul scrubbed clean for Mass on Sunday.

Were there more ways to cook dirty rotten cabbage?
And the endless potatoes as they waited for bacon,
the squealing pig butchered in the yard,
bled into buckets for pudding,
the sad, bad smell clinging to clothes
for the week ahead and beyond.

She rattles a list of duties like a mantra:
foot turf, mind babies, gather kindling,
clean pots, fetch water, dig spuds,
sweep, wash, wring, find, pick, cut, chop.
And all for the lash of the belt, buckle end out
for being loudly mouthy or silently sullen.
Whichever, whatever.

There's a pause as the Barista takes money,
and the coffee arrives here in the present
"Do you ever go back?"
She spreads beautifully manicured fingers,
stands straight in well-cut designer suit,
steady on high heels, tries to smile.
"As if," she whispers, "as if."

Acknowledgements

I am grateful to the following organisations and publications for their validation of my work: Strokestown International Poetry Festival; Hennessy New Irish Writing in the *Irish Times*; *Crannóg Magazine*; *Skylight 47*; *Poetry Ireland Review*.

Some of the poems have been read to audiences in Ireland, at The Dock, Carrick-on-Shannon; Strokestown International Poetry Festival; Listowel Writers' Week; the Hawk's Well Theatre, Sligo; Ballina Arts Centre, Mayo; Charlestown Arts Centre, Mayo; The Irish Writers' Centre, Dublin; Coole Park, Galway; also at several events for Poetry Day Ireland, and at various outings with the Hermit Collective, a group of writers, artists and musicians who put on pop-up shows in the west of Ireland.

In 2017 I was greatly encouraged by winning places on two Poetry Masterclasses, the first with the former National Poet of Wales, Gillian Clarke, and the UK Poet Laureate, Carol Ann Duffy. The second was with Gillian Clarke and Maura Dooley. Both of these Masterclasses were at Tŷ Newydd, the Literature Centre of Wales. I am grateful to the Arts Council of Ireland for a Travel and Training Award which funded my attendance at the second Masterclass.

My thanks are also due to friends at the Word Corner Café at the Dock in Carrick-on-Shannon, County Leitrim. We meet monthly to share the written and spoken word, in the place where many of these poems had their first public outing.